TAKE A CLOSER LOOK AT YOUR

Bladder

BY MARNE VENTURA

Published by The Child's World®
1980 Lookout Drive • Mankato, MN 56003-1705
800-599-READ • www.childsworld.com

Acknowledgments
The Child's World®: Mary Berendes, Publishing Director
Red Line Editorial: Editorial direction and production
The Design Lab: Design
Content Consultant: Jeffrey W. Oseid, MD

Photographs ©: Hemera/Thinkstock, title; Sebastian
Kaulitzki/Shutterstock Images, title; Osokina Liudmila/
Shutterstock Images, title, 23; Sebastian Kaulitzki/
Shutterstock Images, 5; Jupiterimages/Thinkstock, 7, 15, 24;
Shutterstock Images, 9, 12, 13; iStockphoto/Thinkstock, 11;
Blend Images/Thinkstock, 17; Nicole Waring/iStockphoto,
19; Polka Dot Images/Thinkstock, 21

Front cover: Hemera/Thinkstock; Sebastian Kaulitzki/
Shutterstock Images; Osokina Liudmila/Shutterstock Images

ISBN: 978-1623235505
LCCN: 2013931441

Printed in the United States of America
Mankato, MN
July, 2013
PA02175

About the Author

Marne Ventura writes for children in kindergarten through sixth grade. A former elementary school teacher, she holds a master's degree in education from the University of California. Marne has helped to create over 50 software products, apps and books for learning reading, math, science, and social studies. She also contributes stories and articles to children's magazines.

Table of Contents

CHAPTER 1
What Is a Bladder?

The **organs** inside your body are always hard at work. Each organ belongs to a **system** with a special job. Your bladder is an organ in the urinary system. This system filters waste from the blood, which makes **urine**. Your bladder holds the urine until it leaves your body.

Put your hands on your hips. Do you feel the top of your **pelvic bone**? It is shaped like a bowl. Your bladder rests at the bottom of the bowl.

The bladder is made of smooth muscle. Smooth muscles are arranged in layers. The bladder is also an **involuntary** muscle. These are muscles that work without your control. Involuntary muscles do their work on their own. Your stomach muscles are also involuntary muscles.

The bladder is an involuntary muscle that can work on its own.

Your bladder works like a water balloon. As your bladder fills with urine, it stretches to a bigger size. Your bladder goes back to a smaller size after you urinate.

An eight-year-old will make about 1 quart (1 L) of urine every day.

A healthy bladder can hold 16 ounces (473 mL) of urine. That is like a very large glass of water. The bladder is about the size and shape of a pear.

Your bladder can hold as much fluid as a large glass of water.

CHAPTER 2

What Does a Bladder Do?

The urinary system has many parts including the bladder. The system has two **kidneys**, two **ureters**, and one **urethra**. The kidneys are very important. Kidneys filter waste from your blood. These bean-shaped organs are the size of your fist. One kidney sits on each side of your body.

Blood is sent to the kidneys by the heart. The heart is always pumping blood through your body. More than 1 quart (1 L) of blood is sent to your kidneys every minute!

Tiny bundles of blood vessels work inside the kidneys. These vessels clean the blood as it passes through the kidneys. The vessels separate waste, extra water, and salt from the blood, which all become urine.

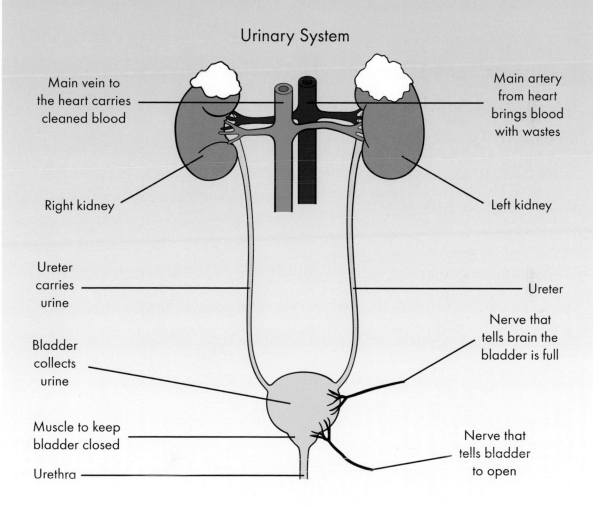

Urinary System

Main vein to the heart carries cleaned blood

Main artery from heart brings blood with wastes

Right kidney

Left kidney

Ureter carries urine

Ureter

Nerve that tells brain the bladder is full

Bladder collects urine

Muscle to keep bladder closed

Nerve that tells bladder to open

Urethra

Urine is made up of four types of waste. One type of waste is made as your body breaks down food. The second type is made as the body breaks down muscle. The third type of waste is **ammonia**, which is a gas your body makes as it breaks down **protein**. The fourth type is a fluid made by the liver called **bile**. Urine also includes water, salt, and a product that makes it yellow called **urochrome**.

Urine leaves the kidneys through one of the ureters. This long tube leads to the bladder. Urine flows down the ureter and into the bladder. The bladder holds the urine until it leaves the body.

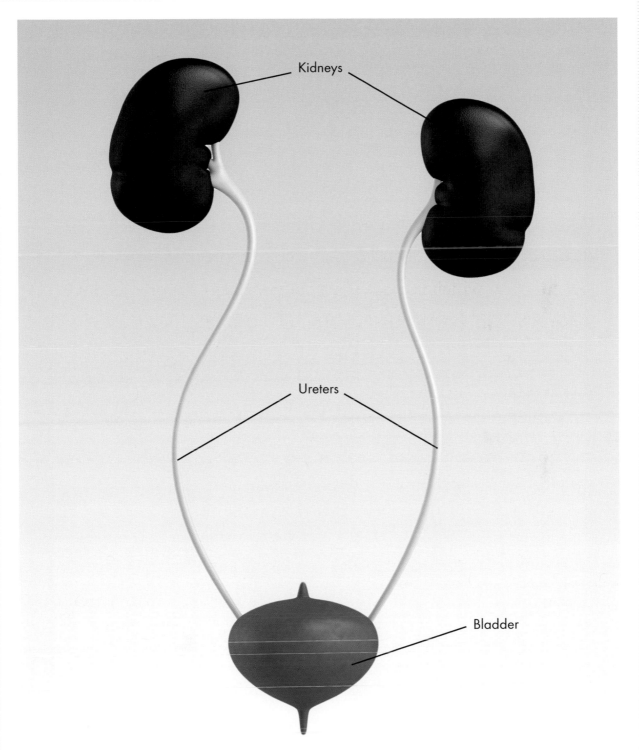

Kidneys

Ureters

Bladder

Urine flows through the ureters on its way to the bladder.

The urethra leads out of the base of the bladder. Two muscles circle the urethra. These muscles work like a rubber band. The muscles keep the urine inside your bladder until you urinate.

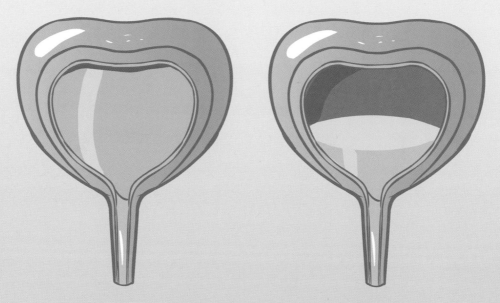

Your bladder muscles hold the urine inside until you go to the bathroom.

Nerves send a signal to your brain when your bladder is full. You feel the need to empty your bladder. Your brain tells the urethra muscles to relax. It tells the bladder muscles to tighten. You squeeze the urine out of your bladder. The urine goes through the urethra and into the toilet.

Your nerves signal your brain when your bladder is full so you know when to go to the bathroom.

CHAPTER 3

Why Do I Need a Bladder?

The bladder is the storage tank for urine. It lets you hold and get rid of urine. As your body turns food into energy, it makes waste. As your body grows and repairs itself, it makes waste. Your kidneys turn waste, extra water, and salt into urine. If waste stayed in your blood, it could make you sick.

A ureter is about 10–12 inches long (25–30 cm) and about 1/8 inch (3–4 mm) in diameter.

The urinary system could not do its job without the bladder. The bladder helps keep your body clean and helps you get rid of waste.

Your bladder helps get rid of all the waste in your body.

CHAPTER 4

Problems with the Bladder

Most bladders work as they should. But sometimes there are problems with the bladder.

A baby's bladder fills and empties on its own. The baby has not learned to control its bladder. Most children's brains learn to control their bladder by four years old. It takes longer for some children to learn control. They might wet the bed at night. Or the child might have an accident during the day. Many things can cause loss of bladder control. Children who wet their beds may have a small bladder. Their bladder gets too full if they sleep for a long time. The nerves going to the brain might still be developing. The bladder muscles might also still be developing. Children usually outgrow bladder control problems. Doctors can provide exercises or lifestyle changes that help.

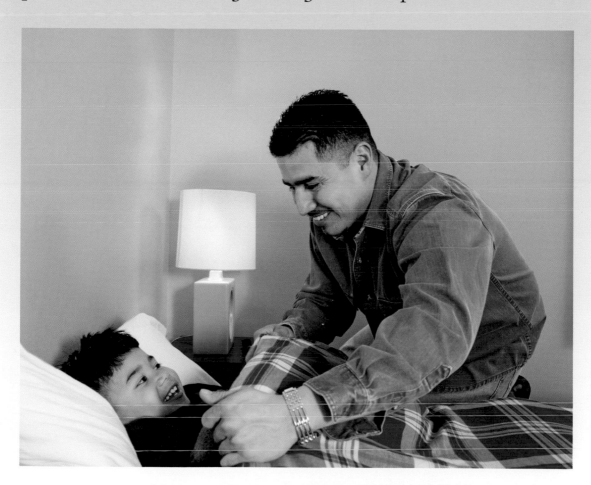

Children usually outgrow bladder control problems when the bladder muscles are fully developed.

Another bladder problem can be caused by an infection. This can happen when germs get inside your body and make you sick.

You might feel the need to urinate more when you have a bladder infection. It might burn or itch when you urinate. Doctors prescribe antibiotics to cure the infection.

At any moment, about one quarter of your blood is in your kidneys.

Sometimes a kidney cannot do its job. Sometimes both kidneys do not work right. Every person needs one working kidney. If both kidneys do not work, surgeons can do a kidney transplant. In this operation a healthy kidney is removed from one person and given to a person whose kidneys are not working. Both people can be healthy if they each have one good kidney.

If both kidneys do not work, doctors can find you a healthy kidney.

CHAPTER 5

Keeping the Bladder Healthy

Taking care of your bladder is easy. There are a few simple rules to follow.

It is important to drink enough fluids. Water is the best choice. Water helps all parts of your body do a better job. It also helps prevent bladder infections. It is important to drink extra water if it is hot outside. If you are exercising, you should drink more water, too.

It is also important to take a shower every day. Try to avoid using bubble bath soap. This soap can cause a bladder infection. Wearing clean clothes is also a good idea. Being clean will get rid of bacteria that might cause a bladder infection. Urinate right away when you need to and empty your bladder completely. This will also help to prevent bladder infections.

Eating fresh fruits and vegetables are also good for your bladder. These foods have a lot of water in them. Fruits and vegetables also have vitamins and fiber that keep you healthy.

Newborn babies are about 78 percent water. By one year old, they are 65 percent water.

It is important to take care of yourself and help keep your bladder healthy.

GLOSSARY

ammonia (uh-MOH-nyuh) Ammonia is a gas made by the body. Ammonia is made when the body breaks down protein.

bile (BILE) Bile is a liquid made by the liver. Urine contains bile.

involuntary (in-VOL-uhn-ter-ee) To have no control over something is involuntary. The bladder is made up of involuntary muscles.

kidneys (KID-neez) Kidneys are two bean-shaped organs. The kidneys filter waste from the blood and produce urine.

organs (OR-guhnz) Organs are groups of tissues that perform a special job. The bladder is an organ in the urinary system.

pelvic bone (PEL-vik BOHN) The pelvic bone is a part of the skeleton that is made up of three hip bones. The bladder sits near the bottom of the pelvic bone.

protein (PROH-teen) Protein is a substance found in all living things. Your body breaks down protein, which creates ammonia.

system (SISS-tuhm) A system is a group of organs or parts that work together. The bladder is a part of the urinary system.

ureters (YOOR-eh-turz) Ureters are the tubes through which urine flows from the kidney to the bladder. Ureters are part of the urinary system.

urethra (YOOR-eth-rah) The urethra is the tube through which urine leaves the bladder. The urethra is the final part in the urinary system.

urine (YOOR-uhn) Urine is fluid waste created by the kidneys as they filter blood. The bladder holds urine until it is released from the body.

urochrome (YOOR-oh-kroh-muh) Urochrome is a breakdown product of the blood. Urine contains urochrome.

LEARN MORE

BOOKS

Cole, Joanna. *The Magic School Bus: Inside the Human Body*. New York, NY. Scholastic. 1989.

Simon, Seymour. *The Human Body*. New York, NY. Smithsonian/Harper Collins. 2008.

Vogel, Julia. *How the Incredible Human Body Works: by the Brainwaves*. New York, NY: Dorling Kindersley, 2007.

WEB SITES

Visit our Web site for links about the bladder: **childsworld.com/links**

Note to Parents, Teachers, and Librarians: We routinely verify our Web links to make sure they are safe and active sites. So encourage your readers to check them out!

INDEX